Zen of the Ox Herder

by Tensho Shûben & Kuoan Shihyan

Introduction and Comments
by Rune Ødegaard

preface by Gustav Ericsson

Zen of the Ox Herder
© Rune Ødegaard 2014

Published by Krystiania
Oslo, Norway

First edition 2014

Cover: Rune Ødegaard & Joachim Svela

ISBN: 978-82-93295-06-8

www.krystiania.com

Zen is to grasp nothingness with experience.

Preface

I had the pleasure to become acquainted with Rune Ødegaard about two years ago, and then to continue and deepen our association. We both have roots in different streams of the Christian tradition - Rune as a Gnostic teacher and me as a Lutheran Minister - while at the same time, to us both, Zen practice is a heart matter. In this regard, it is my experience that Rune's dual belonging is firmly rooted and deeply nourishing to him as a whole person.

As an ordained Zen teacher since 2004, Rune asked me to become his guide in the practice. I gladly agreed, but the truth is that we have supported each other. Ever since the first text Rune sent me, I have enjoyed the warm and down-to-earth clarity of his writing and exploring. We have processed many themes and questions over the months and years of our friendship, and among them some texts related to the ten images and poems of this book.

The ten pictures of the ox herder were among the first impressions that really got through to me when I began studying and practicing Zen. I am not primarily interested in them as a course curriculum or ladder of achievement, but I find myself returning to them again and again. Sometimes I recognize myself in one or several of the pictures, and it often makes me smile. I feel connected to the images and I am happy that Rune's insights are published and made available to anyone interested in Zen practice and life.

My Zen teacher, Gudo Nishijima Roshi, died earlier this year. Throughout his life, his emphasis was on a balanced and humanistic approach to Zen practice, and I believe he would have appreciated Rune's book very much. I hope the reader will return to this book at different times and circumstances in life, and find a refreshing sense of joy and ease on her or his path.

Umeå, Sweden, 2 June 2014

Gustav Ericsson
Lutheran Minister and Hospital Chaplain
Dharma succsessor of Zen Master Gudo Nishijima Roshi

Foreword

I am very fond of pictures and poems that may lead to reflection and self discovery. However my experience working with such artistic expressions derives from my affiliation with the western esoteric tradition and series such as *Splendor Solis*, *Mutus Liber* and *Lambspring*. Nevertheless I am very much aware of the fact that the map is not the landscape. I do rather view series like these as mental photographs from a spiritual journey, a spiritual expedition performed by an individual wishing to give something back to others following the same esoteric path.

The ox herder pictures describe such a spiritual journey using the facade of Zen Buddhism. It is a clean and simple expression inviting reflection and is a key to deepened relationship with the present moment and life itself. They derive from the western image series I know as there is no need to possess extensive knowledge of several esoteric traditions, symbolic languages, myths and secrets in order to be able to access their meaning. The only thing you need is some simple keys and experience with the path.

In this series it may be sufficient to know that the ox herder is yourself as an individual in a process and the ox is your buddha nature. The buddha nature is described in several ways – Zen master Dogen describes it as real reality and existence, and the fulfilment of mortality in emptiness.

I have had help translating the instructions and poems into English, and have worked with the language to make them as beautiful as possible; in this book I present them together with the pictures. Furthermore I have tried to communicate some of my experiences as I have travelled and am still travelling this path. My comments are based upon my collected experience of Zen, Gnosticism and other western esoteric currents as life experience.

I do however not claim any exclusive knowledge, unavailable to other individuals travelling this same path. I do not, as you will see, even claim to keep to a purely Zen kind of genre, if such a thing even exists. My foundation is laid upon a mixture of Zen and Sethian

Gnosticism, and I lean heavily upon Muso Kokushi as I claim that it is possible to convey the spirit of Zen through a multitude of expressions if one has grasped its fundamentals.

My intention with this little book is simply to reach out to whoever desires what is in this hand.

These are my contemplations on the journey with other travellers, a lasting, penetrating, but perfectly ordinary experience – a journey to Nowhere.

Nowhere , the year of the horse, 2014

Rune Ødegaard

To the Zennists,
and all men and women
travelling the pathless path.

Presented at the winter meditation gathering of
Nøkkerozen in 2014

INDEX

Preface	6
Foreword	9
Index	13
Introduction	15
Why a series of pictures?	18
Three processes in one series	20
The journey to the beginning	23
Seeking the ox	24
Comment	26
Ox tracks	32
Comment	34
Discovering the ox	40
Comment	42
The journey towards knowing yourself as one	47
Catching the ox	48
Comment	50
Cultivating the ox	54

Comment	56
Riding the ox home	60
Comment	62
The journey towards knowing yourself as none	65
Man alone	66
Comment	68
Vanished	72
Comment	74
Reintegration	78
Comment	80
The Marketplace	82
Comment	84
Some final reflections	87
Appendix	90
Krystiania publications	101

Introduction

In ancient China the ox was one of the most important domesticated animals performing heavy labour for the farmers. This may be the obvious reason for choosing this particular animal as the main symbol through this series of pictures, representing a wild animal that had been reclaimed. If the pictures had been painted today they might have featured a student in search of online connection. The reality conveyed through these pictures stands the test of time and is as true today as it was in the 1500s when the Japanese Zen monk and abbot of Shôkokuji temple in Kyoto, Tensho Shûbun, painted them.

All the pictures have an instruction and a poem as well. These are attributed to Kuoan Shihyan, a Chinese Zen monk who lived during the Sung dynasty. These texts are collected in the Rinzai handbook Zudokko, *The poison painted drum*. The theme of the instruction and the poem is similar. The poem is more artistically conveyed, and the instruction is more of an explanation even though it may be deemed too cryptic to be understood as an explanation according to our modern standards.

Through my comments on each of the pictures, I try to shed some light on the process depicted.

Why a series of pictures?

Through a series of ten pictures, a possible Zen journey is described step by step. And even by claiming that this is the case the truth of the pictures diminishes. Zen is no journey. There is nowhere to go, there are no steps leading to a particular place and by pointing at pictures in order to describe degrees of attainment, the spirit of Zen may be entirely lost. So why then a series of pictures?

First of all, it is important to highlight the fact that the map is not the landscape. Eating the menu does not make you satisfied. Pictures are static; our human reality is ever changing. Reality is change.

However the pictures may be used as visual aids for teachers as a compass for the solitary student, or as aids to better understand one's own experiences as an unvoiced discussion partner.

I experience the pictures as road signs. Road signs may tell you where you are or where you are heading, but not how to get there, how you

will experience the place or how the journey will be. This depends entirely upon the person travelling and what he or she has brought with him or her as baggage or as past experiences. Diving into Zen is a process, developing from being interested in Zen to becoming Zen.
The series may be more meaningful to people who have travelled the path for some time than for beginners. I have experienced that familiarity with the path gives some perspective of fullness or wholeness, how I connect to the process in the pictures and how to proceed. Thus the pictures and the comments may be of value for those who wish to contemplate their journey thus far, the road ahead and the present situation. My advice is to consult the pictures once or twice a year, and see if they give you some kind of sensation of familiarity or even a lightning flash like *eureka*.
Even though the road is individual, everyone walks alone and how it is perceived is coloured by the events of life, there is something similar in all human lives. With this in mind, I hope these pages may be a true companion for your own journey.

Three processes in one series

There are several ways to work with these pictures; I have chosen to present them as three distinct processes that we meet in our practice. In this way the pictures one to three comprises one process, four to six another, and seven to nine the last process. Picture number ten is the beginning or the end of the full process. This last picture may point to the first meeting between teacher and student and the individual understanding that he is in need of a spiritual journey. The teacher picture may also be relevant to link all the other cards as well. In this case it may be considered a joker card.

I have chosen to call the first process *"The journey to the beginning"*

These pictures describe the journey from becoming aware of a need. This need is understood as the need of a deeper communion with existence itself. It may also be the quest for an understanding of the meaning of life or a wish to assimilate the perspectives of some religion or philosophy. This process culminates when the herder sees the ox. His perspective is then changed from beliefs or faith to pure experience; a Zen encounter. And now faith is connected to experience not merely the hearsay of others.

I have named the second process *"The journey towards knowing yourself as one"*.
This process starts when we have had our first experience with the buddha nature, but it still feels like an external faculty, as if it is something we have to acquire through effort or it has to be fitted into our ego or self understanding.
This process is concluded when we experience that the buddha nature in reality is part of our being; it is our true being. It is one unity. This insight concludes the journey for a great many seekers, as most people truly desire feelings of fullness, consistency and unity, however how fragile they are.
At his stage this state is truly quite fragile, as to keep this condition of oneness requires a continual effort to remain flexible. Our mind still favours thoughts of polarity and we may fall

into stagnation as our mind structures are turned hard with the passing of time.

I have named the last process *"The journey towards knowing yourself as none"*.
This process is initiated when there is no ox and no herder. There is only the human being left, and this man offers his veneration to existence itself. This process annihilates all expectations of a fixed future and all prejudices and nostalgias rooted in the past. It is the pathway to a profound unification with the present, moment by moment.

At the end of this process that has changed everything into being exactly what it always has been, the man in image ten emerges out of the wilderness in order to meet people at the pubs and market.

He is the unexpected buddha.

The Journey to the Beginning

Seeking the ox

Introduction

The ox is not gone, so why do we seek?
Turned from his true nature, all is fragmented:
Gaze in a haze, the fullness forsaken.
Hills of home are fading away,
Crossroad follows crossroad.
Mind entangled in loss and gain.
Thoughts of right and wrong,
rise as swords from the ground.

First poem

Wading and searching the grassland.
Rivers grow and mountains rise tall,
Roads without beginning or end,
Exhausted despair, no tracks to be found.
Solely the song of the mountain cicada in the maple trees.

Comment

The introduction begins by saying:
"The ox is not gone, so why do we seek?"
This leads us directly into the heart of the matter: Why should we spend time looking for something that is not gone?

It is a common interpretation of the pictures that the herder represents the individual seeking insight and the path of true reality. The ox is commonly interpreted as being our buddha nature, our true being.

The question still stands: What is the target of the search and what is the nature of the seeker? The answer to this question is the answer to the self knowledge riddle displayed in these pictures: You are actually looking for yourself. This may naturally lead to the next question: What does this mean? And the answer to this is all the implications of being able to grasp the reality indicated in these pictures.

The point of entry is usually an unease or anguish due to a sincere feeling of lack of understanding.

Nevertheless the first instruction informs you that this is really not the case, the ox is not gone, and you are exactly where you are and you can surely be no other place.
There is nothing wrong with you. Obviously it is easy to state this as a fact if you have had the insight leading you to this conclusion, but for others it will perhaps only seem a hollow statement born of faith or trust at best.
It is as futile as to explain to a claustrophobic that there is no need to be afraid of this very undersized room.

So what should one do if there have not been any understanding of the first instruction, and you have left home for an ox chase and you feel the misery increasing by every step you take into the wilderness? Just look at the boy in the picture. It looks as if his feet are off in a different direction to his upper body. It is pretty clear, looking at the picture, that this boy does not know where to go or where to focus. He has no feeling of fullness and the journey has lost its initial meaning.

This is the status described in the next line of the instructions:
"Turned from his true nature, all is fragmented".
The core problem is that we have turned ourselves away from reality itself and changed it for make believe based upon causalities and connections, a spider's web of polarities, aesthetic and emotional divisions. We have become alienated to ourselves.

Zen tradition has no explicit explanation for how this alienation came to be, but there is no need for understanding of its source as long as we can explore the way out of it. The answer is how we may unshackle ourselves. We seek deeper access to the present moment, the here and now, even as we recognize that allegories and pictures may be of great aid in this work.

The text continues to elaborate on the state of the first picture:

"Gaze in a haze, the fullness forsaken.
Hills of home are fading away,
Crossroad follows crossroad.
Mind entangled in loss and gain.
Thoughts of right and wrong,
rise as swords from the ground."

We have lost our perspective of the totality and the fullness of our being, and as our quest commences, we drift further and further away from our true home, away from ourselves. We trade reality for self created illusions and dreams. The journey leads us to countless crossroads, and the choices and roads seem innumerable. In this chaos of roads and choices, we try to make calculations of cost and benefits, right and wrong, and rather than approaching true reality we delve deeper and deeper into the dream.

The one thing we know for sure in this situation is that we have tried to achieve or clarify matters that we are not even capable of defining. Now it is time to admit to ourselves that we do not even know where we are - we are profoundly lost.

In this insight is a key to the first picture: I face the fact that I have no idea where the ox is. It is not in the stable at home and I do not even have a clue where I am at the present moment.

The situation may give rise to frustration, and in this feeling may be the start of motivation, to stand the ground.

The beginning has been discovered.
Being mentally trapped in the first picture may be compared to being a piece of wood floating in a river. It goes with the current and is totally unaware that the journey in any case leads from sea to sea, and that the water is everywhere all the time...

Ox tracks

Introduction

The scriptures make way for conception.
The tracks are revealed through the teachings.
Obviously all vessels are one,
It is all the same existence.
Unable to discriminate right from wrong,
how can one distinguish truth from lies?
Advancement not yet achieved,
but at least the tracks has been found.

Second poem

Tracks in the river bed and the undergrowth.
Deep in the grassland – can you see it or not?
Deeper and deeper into the mountains,
Its muzzle is raised to the skies,
And nothing remains unseen.

Comment

The person in the picture holds a different posture, no longer do head and feet seem to try to move in different directions.
He has discovered tracks and has gained some focus in his endeavours. Symbolically this may mean that he has decided which philosophy to pursue and who's to be his teacher along the path.
The introduction tells us where he has discovered the tracks:
"The scriptures make way for conception.
The tracks are revealed through the teachings".
After some time in the cognitive wilderness of self knowledge, light is often shed upon the situation by other people who have travelled the same path. These teachings may reveal themselves in the meeting between people or in the meeting between the seeker and the books. This experience may nurture the inspiration of the seeker, and show him that there are others who have followed this path that it leads them to awareness and wakefulness.

Seeing is believing; it is easier to keep on the track knowing others who walk the path besides us or knowing of others in previous times who have fulfilled the same quest.

We have found tracks.

This approach is both right and wrong. Even though he has found an external goal, true knowledge of our buddha nature cannot be acquired outside of our own being or as a theoretical exercise. Even seeking to acquire it may by itself make it harder to grasp. However the external quest may be an important source of inspiration at this early stage of the process. At this stage the seeker may think it is possible to study and learn Zen as though taking a degree at a university. Further experience will in time disclose to the ardent student that the only way to learn Zen is to become Zen, and it is experience not knowledge that opens this gateless gate. Zen is not a theoretical study, even though theory may be required along the way.

In this picture the process is just initiated, but it is truly initiated, and as the tracks have been discovered, the polar star has risen on the horizon. The boy in the picture has acquired some knowledge of the path, but he has little or no experience in the art of walking this trail. The theoretical knowledge has resonated within him as a belief or a fantasy of future attainment. Now it is time to move on from beliefs to knowledge through experience and practice. It is important not to be stranded on the island of faith when the realm of reality may reveal the truth of your hypotheses.

For as long as the teachings remain a hypothesis rather than life itself, the mind will flash between internal – external, right – wrong, high – low and other polarities.

Trying to repress these is of no use and even counterproductive, as they are nurtured and conserved by us trying to push them away. As we focus on doing the right things, the awareness of what is wrong grows greater simultaneously.

The way to disarm this polarity approach is to treat them with non-attachment and tolerant awareness. Everything is as it is! Do not let the ego confuse the tracks into being the animal itself, or dogmas in the scriptures into being reality. The ego does not want the polarities weakened, as it is its primary tool in defining the world and all living things. The ego may even interpret the undifferentiated awareness of *zazen*, Zen meditation, as an attack on its existence. Therefore the ego often reacts by bringing unease and irrational anxiety into the meditative state.

The instruction describes the process in the following manner:

"Obviously all vessels are one,
It is all the same existence.
Unable to discriminate right from wrong,
how can one distinguish truth from lies?".

The status of the present moment is stated at the end:

"Advancement not yet achieved,
but at least the tracks have been found".

The seeker has found a point of entry into the process, but has not yet been able to turn the theoretical perspective into true participation in reality. Due to this, any involvement in the sides of the polarities are, from a certain perspective, equally right and equally wrong. His journey is based upon theory; he is dependent on other people's intellectual charity. His next step is to take part in the knowledge himself.

The second poem confirms that tracks have been found, and the scenery is changing. He is on the track and due to acquired theoretical knowledge the wilderness seems less dense. People at this stage report feelings of enthusiasm and motivation, the spiritual journey turns into a magical romance. It is similar to being in love; everything is fantastic the journey is great. The focus is fixed on everything connected to the process and everything connected to the tradition. There are positive projections going everywhere, towards the teachings, fellow students and towards the teacher.
Phenomena understood to be irrelevant to the work is given less focus and may even be neglected.

Discovering the Ox

INTRODUCTION

Listen and see the entrance.
See through, and see the source.
This is how it is with all six senses,
all actions give way to acquaintance.
It is as salt in water or glue in paint.
Raise your eyes; it is all in this way.

THIRD POEM

The nightingale sings on a branch.
warming sun, soft breeze,
Green willows on the river bank.
No place to run or hide.
Noble head and horns,
inconceivable by art.

Comment

The introduction connected to this picture begins in the following manner:
"Listen and see the entrance".
This instruction points the reader back to picture number two, where we are instructed that the meaning may be discovered through the scriptures. In earlier times these teachings were conveyed orally from teacher to student. Now that most of the teachings are written down, we no longer have to be merely dependent on oral stories.

Are the teachings understood, and do they reflect our reality? If we could grasp what the written word referred to in the living world, this knowledge would open the path. It is not so much a question of secrets and mysteries, as awareness, perspective and insight. The person in possession of these qualities will know that the entrance is hidden everywhere, between here and now, as if forever has been concealed before our very eyes.

This may sound elementary, but the simplest truth is often the most difficult to comprehend. We have a tendency to complicate the simple, not being willing or able to accept its plain characteristic.

When the right perspective has been acquired, a kind of non evaluating perspective, turning our senses towards ourselves, we will be aware of the great or unrestricted self. This is the individual as unconditioned being. The instruction describes it in the following manner: "*See through, and see the source*".

And meeting the ox influences every faculty of our being, all our senses and cognitive structures:

"*This is how it is with all six senses,
all actions gives way to acquaintance*".

This is a point that renders everything transparent and it also gives us an understanding of the insight that everything is part of the so called Source. Usually this event makes way for an urge to connect to this Source, this unrestricted reality.

It may be confusing to experience that everything actually is one and part of the same whole. This boundlessness is in everything there is, *"It is as salt in water or glue in paint. Raise your eyes; it is all in this way"*.

Knowing this in the mind does on the other hand not necessarily mean that it is known to the heart. Having had an insight into the way of things does not necessarily mean that everyday life is viewed in this way at this stage of the process.

The text describes the experience of insight, the lightning like knowledge, of having stood face to face with Truth itself. This is the first meeting with true reality. This is the first encounter with what the ox herder seeks. Does the meeting live up to our expectations? Is it as we thought it to be? Rarely!

Having had this encounter, having seen what we have seen, makes it impossible to un-see what has been revealed. We cannot dry it out of our eyes with a handkerchief. What is, is as it is, and this is really all there is. Now we have to live with this knowledge whether we like it or not. Any ways it signifies a kind of crossroads in life. I have met people who think that this experience concludes the journey and declare themselves masters. Others have founded religions or sects upon their experience and attributed it to divine intervention.

Do not deceive yourself by building a temple of illusions based on a memory of the ox. This is only the end of the beginning.

The Journey Towards Knowing Yourself as One

Catching the Ox

Introduction

For a long time it hid in the wilderness,
today it is discovered.
Difficult to follow its movement.
It yearns for the hills and the grassland,
Steadfast, untamed.
In order to create a concord,
the whip must be applied.

Fourth poem

Grabbing the beast with vigour and might.
Strong, stubborn, unyielding.
High up in the hillside,
deep down in the valley below.

Comment

The ox-mind and the herder-mind are not viewed as compatible with each other.
It may even turn out to be a mental conflict.
- It is hard to see how the insight I gained by discovering the ox may be harmonized with my present life.
The spiritual romance in picture two is definitely stranded on the reef of reality at this stage.
In this situation it is easy to think that the ox has to be subdued, but this would imply that the buddha nature had to be fitted into the limitation of the ego structure.
This work may be accompanied with sorrow or even periods of depression.
John of the Cross, a Christian saint, describes this process as *the dark night of the soul*. Before we met the ox, we were in love with our concepts of the ox and our expectations for the journey or even fantasising about a goal.
Now everything has been taken from us, and all that is left is an unwilling stubborn ox. In fury or

desperation the boy in the picture tries to whip the ox into submission. But by doing this, he actually whips himself.

This meeting could actually be a dance, but the ego experiences it as a battle. It is the resistance of the ego – resistance against existence and reality. It is an instinctive reaction versus the buddha nature.

The ego wants our experiences to be fitted into a frame thus creating a consistent wholeness rather than to let go of the frame. The ego thinks it may subdue the ox. This is an important step, and it will give us a hard time. People reporting no ambivalence when entering this process, probably deceive themselves into believing that they are at this stage.

How working with this process proceeds depends entirely upon our need for control. The underlying theme for this stage is the need for harmonization, and this must be fulfilled upon entering the next stage.

"Difficult to follow its movement.
It yearns for the hills and the grassland,
Steadfast, untamed.
In order to create a concord,

the whip must be applied".
In this image man and ox are tied together and the unification process is under way, even though there is no real unification. They were never really separated…
An immature perspective gives rise to the idea and feeling of a battle.

At this stage persistence is essential and you must be determined to endure to the end. Teachers and a spiritual community may be of assistance in this work, offering guidance and support.
This will however not prevent the process from running hot and cold. This is a process of initiation and old ways have to give way as true reality suddenly or progressively breaks through old structures.
"Grabbing the beast with vigour and might.
Strong, stubborn, unyielding.
High up in the hillside,
deep down in the valley below".

Cultivating the Ox

Introduction

When a thought appears,
others follow closely.
Wake up, and truth surrounds you,
stay asleep and all is false.
The outer has no part in this,
it is born from the mind itself.
Keep the rope tight,
do not turn around.

Fifth poem

Keep the rope and the whip,
the beast may escape you still.
Herd it until it is peaceful and calm,
without the bridle it will follow you of his own accord.

Comment

As the image shows, there is no open discord. The boy and the ox walk together in the same direction. He has come to terms with the experience of the ox. It all looks very harmonious. There are however reasons for caution, as the experience with true reality still is quite fragile and it is not very well integrated. In this state of being we are very susceptible to fantasies regarding the exquisiteness of our spiritual attainment. This may be pride, the need to differentiate oneself from previous teachers and teachings, or dreaming that we at last have come to full spiritual attainment. Experiencing our own accomplishments, we may also be tempted to elevate ourselves above others, thus creating a new duality between what the confused mind could label the society of illuminated and so called ordinary people. This may result in putting the seeker into an even less enlightened state than when he started his journey. At that initial stage we did at least know that we knew nothing. In this process we may lead ourselves to believe that we have fully integrated the buddha nature, even though we have only just discovered it. Illusions and experiences live side by side in our being, and they may both present themselves as moments of clarity and illumination.

The instruction describes this web of thoughts:

"*When a thought appears,
others follow closely*".

As we are involved in actively deceiving ourselves, the ox vanishes or becomes distant. At this stage of dawning enlightenment, it is important to remain true to our experience of reality; we must lead the ox as we follow our experience holding the rope of reality. Or we can turn around and sleep on the bed of ego created make believe. Remaining a self proclaimed king or buddha, we risk viewing our experience with the ox as so unique that it exceeds the experiences of all others, or whatever pleases a dreamer.

It is our personal choice, and the responsibility is entirely ours:

*"Wake up, and truth surrounds you,
stay asleep and all is false.
The outer have no part in this,
It is born by the mind itself".*

I have worked with men and women, who truly believe that this is the end of the journey, but remember that we are only halfway through the series.

– so:
*" Keep the rope tight,
do not turn around.*

Riding the ox home

Introduction

The struggle is over,
gain and loss bear no meaning.
Humming a simple tune, playing a tune.
Riding the ox,
resting the eyes on nothing at all.
If called for, it will not turn around.
If restrained it will not stop.

Sixth poem

Riding the ox,
riding calmly home.
The tune dissolves the evening light.
Feelings relax with each rhythm and verse.
In tune with each other – no need for words.

COMMENT

This is the most famous picture in the series. In China you may buy figurines and posters of the boy riding the ox. The popularity of this picture may be connected to the harmonious display. Most of the instruction describes this harmony. Firstly: *"The struggle is over"*.
This is fundamental; but there is something else in this setting, a playful simplicity and peacefulness:
"Gain and loss bear no meaning.
Humming a simple tune, playing a tune.
Riding the ox,
resting the eyes on nothing at all".
There has been a stabilization of the more balanced harmony between the boy and the ox, it is the first indication of a unity. There is no whip in this image.
"If called for, it will not turn around.
If restrained it will not stop".
At this stage of the process we may relax and let life itself present its course, trusting that the road will lead us to wherever we are going.

The world is no longer perceived as fragmented and unclear, and we trust that all roads lead to our home.

It is this tranquil mental state many seekers request when they begin their spiritual journey and many will describe this as the goal itself. This is the feeling of peace having regained ability to view ourselves as one whole existence. Thus this picture concludes the journey towards knowing oneself as one.

At this stage theory is turned into experience, and what we have gained is a rediscovery, not a development towards something new. We know our own nature.

In picture three we see the ox for the first time, and we know it to be authentic reality. In this picture we are safely connected to our personal experience of living with the ox as in a harmonious relationship.

So why does the picture series not end here? For many who access this stage of the process, the series ends here.

The dangers connected with remaining at this sixth stage and ending the process here are stagnation and fixation. These may gradually turn into an energy draining enterprise, where the individual tries continuously to relive the fixed nostalgic harmony. As the grasp becomes more and more desperate, the power of the dualities grows stronger and stronger, comparing now to the "good old days". Where there once was a vivid presence there is now only a memory of a fading light.

This fixation is always followed by leaving regular practice. The individual tells himself that he, from this time on, will live the wonderful mystery through everyday life, and then resurrects life as he lived it before he went looking for the ox. Thus we unknowingly disconnect ourselves by drifting back into oblivion.

This is what may be called *useless Zen*: - I have an ox, it is in the stable, I never visit it, but I remember it as I saw it several years ago when I placed it there.

The Journey Towards Knowing Yourself as None

MAN ALONE

Introduction

There are not two realities,
And the ox is only an allegory;
the snare is left when the hare is trapped,
the net is discarded when the fish is caught.
As gold from the dross,
Or as moonlight through the skies;
the lonely beam shone,
before time immemorial.

Seventh poem

The ox bore him to his mountain home.
The ox is no more, you are home.
The sun is already rising,
but dream on.
Rope and whip is at rest in the stable.

Comment

The rest of the journey is the movement from being one to becoming none; this is truly to become the movement and the vital moment. The rest of the process is dedicated to the realization of the buddha nature, not only living in harmony with it. This last journey requires some maturity. This may be allegorically presented as apple trees ripe with fruit. When the fruit is matured it will fall from the tree of its own accord. In the last process nothing is to be acquired it is rather a question of whether you are able to let go. As far as I know this process cannot be initiated by will power alone. The process begins when the seasoned seeker has been riding the ox for a considerable amount of time, and still continues to practise with awareness. Practising zazen, zen-meditation, is an excellent praxis for a lifelong purpose. There may still be need for a teacher, but at this stage the teacher is more like a therapist than a tutor.

To become this movement, Zen can no longer be something we do, it has to be what we are …

In this picture only the human being remains. This does however not mean that the ox is lost yet again. In this picture the process of unification is complete. The unification is fulfilled. There can be but one reality:
*"There are not two realities,
and the ox is only an allegory"*.
If the focus had remained on the buddha nature it would not have been possible to integrate it into our understanding of ourselves. The ox is now on its way to become a natural part of life, it is nothing special. Do not let it become or remain a curiosity in your being, it is just being.

Acknowledging that everything is as it is, in and by itself, man kneels down in prayer. But what is there to pray to when everything is one?
In the next part of the instruction an important part of the process is presented:
*"the snare is left when the hare is trapped,
the net is discarded when the fish is caught"*.

It is important not to be dependent on the means nor be bound by nostalgia or similar feelings. Do what is necessary in order to know the ox, and leave what you no longer need as you travel the path towards the goalless goal. Be an ox herder when you herd the ox, and let this identity go when you no longer perform this function.

The work is to let go of our need of attachments and to be possessive. This does not mean that you should get rid of your belongings, friends and family, but to release and liberate ourselves and others in our relations with them.

What is it in you that preserves this possessiveness? What is it in the present moment?

Investigate the capacity you use to conserve the roles you play with other people and with yourself. How important is it to keep up appearances and preserve your multiple masks? Is it possible to stop pretending? Or do we have to present ourselves and our lives in certain ways? What is there to present?

Up to this stage in the process, Zen-riddles, myths and initiations may have been of great aid, but at this point even these tools have their limitations.

Has there been a development? To this the instruction answers as follows:
"As gold from the dross,
or as moonlight through the skies;
the lonely beam shone,
before time immemorial".

The journey is a voyage to Nowhere, but our perspectives are totally transformed along the path. Existence still remains as it has always been, one and unchanged.

VANISHED

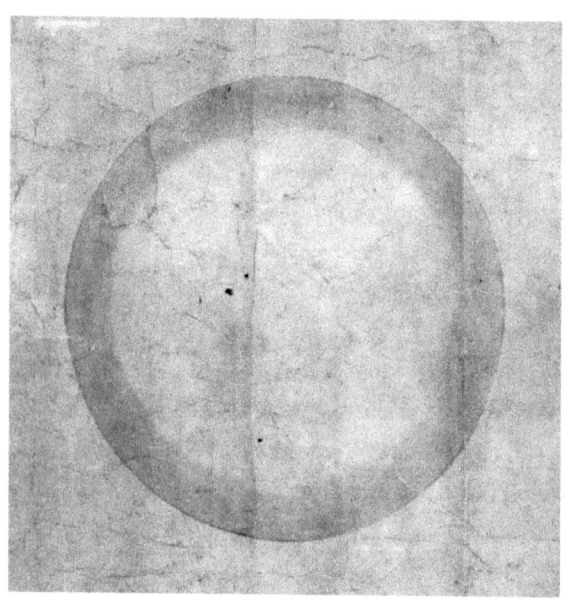

Introduction

The forces of the world are cast away,
thoughts of sanctity have no fullness.
Not being where Buddha lives,
quickly passing where He is not,
if we do not dwell with any of these,
the thousand eyes will scarcely see us.
A thousand birds with flower offerings,
have no value here.

Eighth poem

Rope and whip, man and ox,
are both gone.
The vast inconceivable blue sky.
Snow crystals cannot survive the fireplace.
Now you know what the masters meant.

Comment

In this picture the transformation takes place, the change of perspective from being one to being none.
"The forces of the world are cast away".
At this stage of the process, there is no obsessive identification and no compulsive relations. Whatever comes our way is recognized as it is. It is a spontaneous interaction and then we let go. There is not even an identification with the buddha nature – it is a neither/nor state of mind. It is a process of emptying inner structures. The "I", that was seeking the ox and the ox itself do not really exist as objectives, independent and actual categories and beings. It is as master Dogen told his teacher:
"Body and mind have fallen away".
This did not mean that he was dying or was on the brinks of losing his mind – this was when his teacher acknowledged him as ready.

"Not being where Buddha lives,
quickly passing where He is not,
if we do not dwell with any of these".
Those who have come to this stage in the progress have even left the concepts of buddha, initiation, progress, enlightenment and the mystery. They do not have any meaning at this stage of the process.

Zen may be described as grasping nothingness with experience. Now this is possible.

Here the Zennist dips his quill in nothingness and draws an eternity.

The instruction continues as follows:
"the thousand eyes will scarcely see us [here]", not even the bodhisattva of compassion.

For here is all attachment extinguished, all that is left is unrestricted reality and love. Love with no intended receiver or any object.

"A thousand birds with flower offerings,
have no value here".

This description is in memory of Niutou Fajung, a Chinese monk that was so pious that even the birds offered him flowers. Interestingly they stopped doing this after he had been taught by the fourth Zen patriarch.

Allegorically flowers are offered to the individual who has become one, but not to those who have become none, and if flowers were offered to them it would have been of no consequence to the receiver; it may even hurt the development of those offering them, giving way to projections and fantasies rather than clarity and light.
There is nothing in this picture but the frame. This is a circle or a classical *enso*-circle.
It may be the boundlessness containing all or the complete nothingness, and this may be presented as the very same thing…

This is the extinguishment, a great inner death, as we live with still greater intensity and awareness.

REINTEGRATION

INTRODUCTION

Pure and noble from the beginning,
without any stain at all.
Resting in the unconditioned,
observing life and death.
No fantasy phantoms.
What is there to transform?
Blue water and green mountains.
Observing the rhythm of life.

NINTH POEM

Returning to the source and the spring,
did the work have any cause,
better to be blind and deaf,
in a cottage without view.
The water follows its course,
flowers are red when they blossom.

COMMENT

This is the culmination of the third process. After the extinguishment, when the redemption is fulfilled in nothingness, the great awakening or awareness appears. The individual is still in the world, but sees through everything.

"Pure and noble from the beginning,
without any stain at all.
Resting in the unconditioned,
observing life and death.
No fantasy phantoms".

There is awareness and peace, and no unease or fearfulness connected to his presence in the world. It is rather a communion with everything that makes everything nothing special; and when nothing is special everything is special! There is nothing to purify or transmute, everything is as it has always been. The only difference is that everything is apparent, untied and acknowledged.

"What is there to transform?
Blue water and green mountains.
Observing the rhythm of life."

Everything is ever in a process of change, but in acknowledging reality, no harmful attachments are made. Everything is as a river, ever flowing. It is eternity flowing through your present moment.

"Better to be blind and deaf".
This does not mean that being crippled is a blessing in disguise. It is when hearing and seeing do not give rise to conditioning. When we hear, it is only hearing; when we see, it is only seeing. There is no subjective seeing or hearing. What this really means is the actualization of the process shown forth in this picture.

So, has the journey been a waste of time?
Well, the journey was never a journey, so what is then to be wasted?
There is truly no subject having the experience, as what is; is just as it is:
"The water follows its course,
Flowers are red when they blossom".

THE MARKETPLACE

Introduction

He closes the gate to his cottage,
not even the thousand sages know him.
He hides his light in his own knowledge,
contradicting earlier sages' tracks.
Entering the marketplace with pumpkin bag,
rests against his staff and returns to his home,
confers buddhahood to bartenders and fish
vendors.

Tenth poem

Entering the market, bare breasted, no shoes.
Covered in ashes and mud, with a smiling face.
Displays no mysteries of gods or magicians,
dead trees blossom once again.

Comment

This image may be the beginning or the end of the series depending on identification with the man or the boy.

Here the boy, who has fulfilled the journey, has become a man. He is an enlightened man aiding a young boy. He is a pilgrim liberated from prejudices and expectations.

*"He closes the gate to his cottage,
not even the thousand sages know him.
He hides his light in his own knowledge"*.

He is the personification of redemption, the stranger. No one knows if there are any limitations to the eternity he knows in his own being.

"contradict earlier sages' tracks".

A buddha does not follow the lead of others, but is like an artist expressing himself exactly as he does. He will be your guide, walking the path with you until you are able to be your own guide.

Zen master Muso Kokushi says that a Zen master is independent of all customs, forms and methods. The method and the expression of the tradition have to be born in the meeting between individuals.

The encounter with the sage may just as well take place in a pub as in a beautiful zendo or temple with golden statues.

"Entering the marketplace with pumpkin bag, rests against his staff and returns to his home, confers buddhahood to bartenders and fish vendors".

This part of the instruction does also remind us of Jesus who chose to surround himself with prostitutes and money lenders. It is not the healthy who are in need of medicine.

He is Hanshan, Cold Mountain, visiting the Kuoching temple, a peculiar laughing sage teasing and arguing with the monks.

He is the untraditional teacher disclosing his knowledge on stones and walls as short poems; and meeting the people in the market and in the pubs, everyone awakes to reality. This is not due to his powers or his specific methods. It is rather he just being himself in their presence. Everyone is deeply moved in the encounter with this artist of life itself, and he is presenting himself in innumerable shapes and forms through time. Only through awareness are we able to behold what really is, or as it is said in the Christian scriptures: Let those who have an ear hear.

SOME FINAL REFLECTIONS

I had a presentation trying to convey my understanding of this series of pictures at a meditation gathering in Hallingdal in Norway early in 2014. This made me aware of a potential danger for anyone seeking the *ox process* or its equivalence in the Western esoteric tradition. I want to add this to this text so that my readers may contemplate it on their own or together with other teachers of these spiritual paths. My experience as teacher and guide has only lasted for ten years, but I have even in this relative short time had some important experiences.

The point I want to make is connected to picture three, the first experience with the ox. The problem is that some seekers who enter this stage automatically think they have entered picture six, riding the ox home. At the same time or after a short time these seekers think themselves to have entered process number ten, but then considering themselves to be miracle workers and teachers with remarkable powers.

It is this *process-jumping* that I would like to address. According to my experience with the Western esoteric tradition in general and the Gnostic schools in particular, great emphasis is placed upon how to get to picture number three, how to discover the ox.
Very little has been said about the further process other than how to recognize the adept or sage according to his or her qualities.
I think that several seekers push themselves into the frame with the herder riding the ox, hoping that just thinking they are there will gradually put them there. I think this is an important source of frustration and unhappiness - a sort of charade in order to keep up appearances.
This may be a natural reaction when considerable energy is invested in an endeavour not giving an apparent return on the investment.
I do not think that this is a conscious strategy, but rather the sad result of a natural process poorly described to the seeker.
The third process is also, according to my knowledge of it, also too poorly presented, except through obscure riddles and

unintelligible pictures luring the seeker into a regression process based upon years of studies of contradicting symbols and myths. According to my experience this process puts picture ten on a pedestal and the lost seeker makes the process-jump trying to be what he has yet to experience. It is the believers' way of faking it until you make it.

So I appeal to your introspective ability, to evaluate your possession and work from time to time, and do not deceive yourself. Do not lose the ox as you are occupied with your own expectations of benefits rather than experiencing what is in our interaction with reality as it is.

Appendix

The pictures of Pu Ming

There are several versions of the ox herder pictures. There are similarities and it is very probable that they describe the same process. In this book I attach the images and verses of Pu Ming as they appear and I will let them speak for themselves. This series was published by Chu Hung in 1609. It became popular in Europe and America when included in the *Manual of Zen Buddhism* by D. T Suzuki.

Untamed

A savage ox with pointy horns

Rushing through mountains and valleys

Dark clouds enfold the valley

Who knows what plants are trampled down

TRAINING INITIATED

Rushing a rope through its nose
It resists and I use the whip
Resisting with all its might
But the boy will not yield

Restrained

Restrained the ox comes to rest

It follows through rivers and land

The rope is still kept tight

Vigilant without thoughts of rest

TURNED

The training succeeds and the ox is turned
Its wild and uncultivated will has found peace
But the boy does not yet trust the ox
The ox is still tied with the rope to a tree

TAMED

Under green willows by an old river

The ox is released and left to its pleasures

As the evening mist is covering the fields

The boy returns home together with the ox

Unbound

The ox is peacefully resting
Whip and rope are forever left
The boy is also at ease under a pine
Joyfully playing a serene song

EVERYTHING IS AS IT IS

The sunset illumines the willows by the river
A light mist is covering the fields
It eats and drinks when it is hungry and thirsty
Untroubled the boy is slumbering on the rock

ALL IS FORGOTTEN

The white ox is covered in clouds
Both man and ox are both serene
Moon shadow through clouds is white
Clouds travel east the moon to the west

ALONE IN THE LIGHT

The ox is gone and the herder is his own master
A lonely cloud drifting among the peaks
He is clapping and singing in the moonlight
One barrier left between here and his home

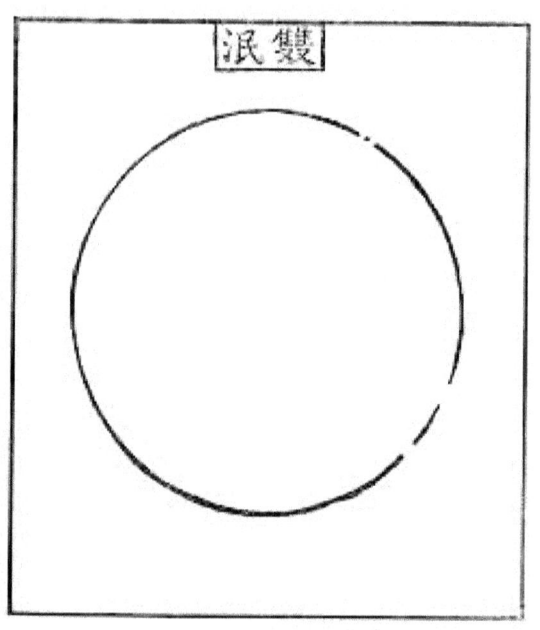

BOTH GONE

Man and beast are both gone
No moonlight shadow in the void
And what is the meaning of all this
See the flowers and grass in the wilderness

Krystiania Publications

Ødegaard, Rune: Nøkkelen: Sethiansk gnostisisme i praksis 2009

Svela, Ove Joachim: Kabbalah: Vestens levende mysterietradisjon 2010

Ødegaard, Rune: Corpus Hermeticum 2010

Ødegaard Rune: Salomos Oder 2011

Ødegaard, Rune: The Key: Sethian Gnosticism in the postmodern world 2011

Ødegaard, Rune: The Gate: Sethian Gnosticism in the postmodern world 2012

Nykland, Sølvi: Noreas Bok: Drømmer om døden og skapelse 2013

de la Croix, Désir: Martinistordenen Ordre Reaux Croix 2013

Ødegaard, Rune: Veien er Zen: Bodhidharmas lære 2013

Ødegaard, Rune: Porten: Sethiansk gnostisisme i praksis 2013

Evjen, Knut: Teofobi: Den gudfryktiges åpenbaring 2013

Ødegaard, Rune & Lindalen, Turi: Frostfjell: Zen-poesi fra fjellet 2013

www.ingramcontent.com/pod-product-compliance
Ingram Content Group UK Ltd.
Pitfield, Milton Keynes, MK11 3LW, UK
UKHW022208230426
12048UKWH00016BA/720